Houses Dim

Will Daunt

First printed and published in 2000 by
Grendon House
8 Laxay Isle of Lewis HS2 9PJ UK

Copyright © Will Daunt 2000
All rights reserved

ISBN 1 898891 16 8
British Library Cataloguing in Publication Data.
A catalogue record for this book is available from the
British Library

Acknowledgements

Poems in the collection have
appeared in *'Smoke'*, *'Orbis'*, *'Pennine Platform'*,
'The Green Book', *'Sepia'*, *'Iota'*, *'Krax'*, *'Period Piece
and Paperback'*, *'Poet's England (Lancashire)'*,
'Poetry North-west' and *'Voices'*.

For *Margaret*

CONTENTS

Houses Dim	4
Above an Ice Fjord	5
Mist Over Eigg	7
Boarders From Luing	8
To Lofoten	9
Islands By Tide	10
Unst ...	11
Other Foulas ...	12
Demolishing The Coal Place	13
Belgian Journey	15
Ronaldsay's Wall	17
From Brussels Airport	18
Maydanek	19
1979	20
Lesson In Loneliness	21
Lent-in-Mendip	22
Not Giotto	23
Where He Fell	24
Living In Lancashire	25
Motorway	26
White Settlers	27
Halfway	28
The Upside Town	
Ormskirk Borders	29
Lost One	30

*It's about time
we were not far from here,
in landscapes
that blind into dusk, onto dawn.
When heart-to-hot
we have our world, in the clear,
many places
that show what we feel, growing warm.*

***

HOUSES DIM

off the gravel side
where this varicose tip
records Fair Isle.

Fog shakes out coughs
over blasty wrecks to Orkney,
each is counted.

Dusk, a shrunk infection
slips in white to stripe the village.
Every metre.

Blustered with its breath,
this pulse will see another summer dim

where houses were.

***

ABOVE AN ICE FJORD

West Greenland

This was the death pad. We squat by;
somewhere to truss up belief like an Inuit,
follow it over like waste or a sledge dog,
down ice-sheets and slobber. That was their way.
Brittle elders judged themselves - embalmed
by the grin of winter - food for the pelt.

Others, of course, crept out of life, watching
from boulders this slithered outcrop.
Wobbling there now gives a quick blink of skull,
then barks from a bluish fox hollow the heart.
She is another who follows the hunger tracks
down to Ilulissat. Heads are a first find -

in shrouds of mosquitoes.
Here with our cameras and clumsy conjectures,
we wonder how, in the splutter of daylessness,
parent and friend excused muscle and petrified
bone at the precipice; afterwards, useless flesh
nuzzled between floes. Now, in their denim,

descendants stalk girls in estate cars,
with empty guns. Cotton-lined dole is the back-
bone that shapes any dog-hauls.
Beyond the freezers and K.G.H. export stores
carcasses lie incarcerated, toyed with
in faltering Danish by bloated hands.

These, by their newest graves grow plastic sprays,
over this grinding intestine:
the ice fjord. As every lost iceberg
escapes with a ricochet, mortuaries
of the mind unfreeze, scraped like a landscape,
cast in this plaster - a modern death mask.

***

MIST OVER EIGG

Enough has come to come away,
a smokescreen holds the hill.
Roofs will rust and stoves can blaze
with brambles. Sedge and heather
come like a cloud below the outcrop,
low enough to soak a living.

Nowhere to drive. The outlines of van
and trailer last, where Gaelic
marks the summit, headlands, lochs,

every signpost now awry.

Visitors largely the want the way
to sands that sing. Enough have come
to flush out history:

mist over land, becoming enough.

***

BOARDERS FROM LUING

Over a sound, there bleed
commuters, awkward and spun
out of land by the pick axe.

They are old bodies of slate
who learn of a past
where the whirlpool sings.

Parting is peat-blunt
and hills throw a shroud.

Seamless, it dribbles
the tide race down,
a ferry of memory
for homesteads to foster.

**

TO LOFOTEN

The islands end.
Vaeroy, a couple of spines,
strains alone
in the rhythmic swell
of memory.

There a man reels
on the main ridge
and scuffed slopes yawn.

Mosken looks anyone's village
and cowers,
with barbed wire gardens
and dropping ways.

Wracks and sheep
crowd the landing shell,
where showers of gulls
cry threats
of possible squall.

The telephone line
sags down on the track
to the settlement,
loaded like hardship.

Its hovels are largely
havens for unanswered calls.

***

ISLANDS BY TIDE

gain phones which bind their ringing shores
with words, unstuck or unexpected.
Polarised, like rain or sunset,
now they are never being away.

When messages land, they're elongated
as fragile planes. The subsidies
have to hold, uncrease affection
and as channels
are vaster than kelp there, meshed by weather.

Each island talks of threatened waves,
with causeways like a root, but sodden.
The contact is somewhere,
almost listening,
yet it brings queries, costs the evening.

And days become hard to recall,
like a dialect gone (but good for quoting),

or unknown skerries, stacks of peat,
an empty school, the sloshing causeway.

They have been daily washing away.
***

Unst: the opposite end of Shetland,
once a thundered war of gods.
At Hermaness and Saxavord
a hurling out of holms from Unst.

Unst - the one portentous thud
of undercarriage or waterline tyre.
Unst, where vowel and boundary drown
at Uyeasound or Burrafirth.

Unst - a time encroached by verge
the radar over folding plains;
unsung, as thrusts on headboards
stunned with almost mustered cries.

***

OTHER FOULAS

wait beyond us -
fear or ardour,

stricken heather,
death by sliding,

the unended
skua squadron

to defy. Pulled
while straining

from the Mainland
who will make it,

in that passage
to the last quay?

The vague isles lie
adrift again,

wheeling with fools.

***

DEMOLISHING THE COAL PLACE
A Deserted Village on DisKo Island, Greenland.

Poised around a summer harbour,
went the light, dividing silence.
Splintered bergs were slinking through
up Vaigat and the Gulf Stream.

We saw a docile ashiness
that rolled against moraines down there,
sculling the straggled inlets
where seals dodged a skinning.

Kayaks, hoisted to that shore,
hung safe as their posterity.

Saqqaq buzzed with hearty children
gutted halibut and dog sleighs.
K.G.H.'s dried provisions
held out credit, fed our guides

then supplied a small boat
turning back to where the coal lay.

Europe's food, stuffed round the outboard
steers to another mess of homes.
Windows blow through seasons here
like history, without the coal.

Paunchy volunteers, we pull up
borrowed wood and burgled compounds.
Greeting visitors and autumn,
we roll down the roof and mountain

and, at a loss for twenty days,
we unearth souvenirs.

Then the partition falls, light shuts in
the expertise, the lie
we work to end. Unleashed dogs
hang as the best hope of culprits;

like a gutted heart, the village
beats out a lone twelfth year.

***

BELGIAN JOURNEY

Returning to the poplar rows,
you straddle Flanders' dykes and farms
where seasons flood and circle Bruges
or hoist their shade like skewed tarpaulins
up the line that pegs Cologne.
You read like an unfranked letter -
flung through stations, blinking where
those market stalls are huddled.

The capital is shouting space,
where villas borrow millions
to warm up art in Horta's shell.
Meanwhile, Schaerbeek and Leuven slip
as trains mingle their languages.

Beyond the Ardennes' turning point,
do not miss each stiffening winch,
its bloated slag. Drunk without work,
that Gueze slugged late in Charleroi
has barely raised a Belga haze.

Avenues here hide unsold lives,
while contours are catching themselves
beside the Semois. At Bouillon
there's game enough to forget
how forests wound the railway up.
They swallow trout and tether boar
they're lost as limestone fissures dripping
the currency of the nation.

That Belgian dash tried England too -
like something pulled from the wardrobe -
tried without fashion,
found in another land that's clashing.

***

RONALDSAY'S WALL

Northern Orkney

Better than maps is the awkward way,
late and unheard;
Islanders bump in and stutter through hay.

Coming this far, the perimeter
(bent in the lens)
seems to have aged; but sheep recur.

When walking here (behind the sea
and turned inland),
the dyke returns, raised listlessly.

And those alive are bred by drift-weed,
like nobbled lines
or thresholds.

                    Crofters working up the food
have measured out ways of how to farm,
where others scrounge;
here bleats an indistinct, oily charm,

and even the vanishing rotors of death
have endpoints
that run when rusty, or grasp for breath.

***

FROM BRUSSELS AIRPORT

You flew out while we were getting fatter.

Hard as departures, the vast tarmac
had a language. We couldn't translate
the kapel under flares, trucks that sneaked
about the maternally-bulging planes;
we missed the ad's as long as cafes,
saw no visor where we looked through.

Zaventum sniggered as you taxied,
subtitled flyovers, suburbs, home.

***

MAYDANEK

Concentration Camp, Eastern Poland

Look - the picture of our guilt
at black-on-green Maydanek.
Toured-to-death we fear the rain
and less,
and then start running
into peace-talk,

I forget how many times.

Look, we wonder at the flat huts' scheme,
their ordered stain
over who they held: blue clouds
over peeled white paint - gas skies
on no man's land.
Granulated magic

I forget how many times.

Look at the random slippers here,
they run to thirty thousand,
distinguished by the lines of sweat,
and piles of wetter times.

Westerners walk through guilt
in uncremated shoes,

so ghosts get killed,

I forget how many times.

***

1979

Showers were toppling the angular clump,
old walls over contours, those breaches
and arms throughout Shropshire.

They rolled in like assonance, shading
alliterative dusks and the ditches
that winter had slurried.

You were there, trying to stand
with a faltering drift underfoot
like the thickness of word.

Sentences trailed beyond Wilderhope,
melting that whiteout to fields
which emerged with the decade.

***

LESSON IN LONELINESS

Salisbury Plain

Imagining Imber, we remember
roads unstringing
half the Plain, wheeling orderlies
each September to vacant beds.

Autumn there, unstaunched and hungry
croons a warning,
like the shelling of an arc
that holes a crater. Something balked

from plough to padlock;
here's the chart of a stricken ward,
its walls collapsing.
Summer shakes up American Road

ricocheting with prose, rebuilt, redrafted.
Those who need the work, engrave it
like a pillbox, for their teachers.
There they wait, our younger Imbers.

***

LENT-in-MENDIP

Here's a butt for weeks on end,
where the barrows weave a sackcloth.

They are leaden flues, like carbines
emptying their ore around us.

Roofs are kneeling in the tinder,
burning from inside, the trauma.

Trees that stand, like buttresses
hide the homeless weeks on end.

Wilder still, a stranded trig point
spans the aimless growth, the slag pits,

All recalls more glowing flora
and the weeks on end, the trauma.

***

NOT GIOTTO

Cometprobe, 1986

Beams though valleys
have threaded us here
while night grew;

bruised out of day-synch and silken,
probes of ours lie stitched in tight.

Meanwhile, Halley
is unzipping wildly
seventy years;

jangled, his shrapnel
flails an unpatterned world-scheme,

resetting dials. Watchers
curse the scrapped decades -

yet we hoard days.
***

WHERE HE FELL

The Captain's House

His yellow house leaves rope enough
to hinge upon.
Its door swings like cartilage
on dusted bone.

His children's kids touch up and scrape
the plastering;
a last emulsion hangs, like home,
without, within.

The firebeds, his flowerplace
may glow again,
but only as an ageing post
for younger men.

Hints of where his colour held
forever fade,
and decades fall to penetrate
a mustard shade.

***

LIVING IN LANCASHIRE

A couple of hundred meals
from how
we came to see that home was wrong,

the seven snub north-west years
that oddly
bleed to distance, far from where?

as cold in the southernmost reach
for those
perspiring from the northern side,

the cover of family, worn
or worse,
the grief that widely doesn't arrive.

Would it be less than better
at twice
a horizon's length, in a vacuum

somewhere outside England,
no nearer
the furthest vanishing point,

but more than neutral
at home
and less foreign, through novelty?

***

MOTORWAY

The new river drains a city,
sliproads suck the pasture.
Blackness.

Like a spillage, the new traffic
buries time, to roar
at midnight.

No-one wonders at the flux of dead air
on a verge to nowhere,
rusting sideways.

Stuffed with flotsam, the new speeds
vent many senseless -
grass ungrazed,

no muck-spred comfort, in the new-stained
clapped-out fear
of tarmac shadow,

printed to death. Day renews the black meanders
on white lines.
Limbs dissolve.

***

WHITE SETTLERS

West Lancashire

A white farm in a kink of land
is the tabletful of what we hope

and where a planed-out charm injects,
from the level Moss, sliding under rain.

An unmade road, like a teenage arm,
cradles everywhere we never drive,

the wall of calm by the sepia field
looks bleached, like home, with the mortgage paid.

That hooked-on harm of twenty-five years
is a punctured sleep where the sky lies down,

where name and number are well alarmed,
and spike what we'd like with who we are,

like a dream of farms. Think of a trip,
recall where the memories cannot start,

and you're here, lying. Sweat runs, from palm to palm
pushing land and youth and home apart.

***

HALFWAY

Clamber up the railway ridge
and see, at half your final age,
the rungs which trod a life of scrub

and wonder when the best (and worst)
pulled out. It's linear
and poorly used, this landscape,

half of seventy years,
a flopped out, filleted
lying down. Hackneyed axes

of pen, paper, line, land,
seize up at the station space

in stationary ageing.
***

THE UPSIDE TOWN

1/1/96

from the Beacon's brow
was a galaxy of lights below.

As dusk elapsed on New Year's Day,
the apertures and time delays
could not expand or give the lie
to that grey template of the sky.

The new town, lit up, slid indoors,
like a star-flung sea, on broken shores.
***

ORMSKIRK BORDERS

And on a rise
of roots and moss,
the quarry ends,
well overrun.

A sandstone town
was unearthed here,
its paths disperse
towards elsewhere.

Some underpin
an upland arc,
where fields succeed
or towns might be,

and others merge
where railways died,
on mounds that lie
like boundaries.

Behind all this
goes Lancashire.
The farms run down
the walls are wide,

and where it lay
it ends, and there
where sunsets rise
the city flares.

***

LOST ONE

Weeks From Safety

You had been weeks
in the blizzard,
where your freeze-frame
left us, parents
on the scanner,
people, warmer
near your icy,
drifted portrait.
Two dimensions
screened your body,
while the widened
world was noisy,
shaking sonar
through the fissures.
Life, the abyss,
half-filled itself.
Your measured head
was buoyant, broad,
your bound-up limbs
were inches long.

A Colder Birth

A clattering
of beds, befores
and afters, last
minutes living,
took him beyond
becoming old.
We rolled away
from chatter, down
maternity's
embankment. Strange,
the simple words
miscarried there;
there, as comfort
strung together.
Then the scuttled
disconnecting:
life, like a plug,
tugged out, sucked in,
and hanging down
and helpless, there.

Disconnecting

That night, I drove
whole cranes away,
ultimate hopes
swung over him,
his closure in
a colder birth.
That year soon lost
the Christmas trees,
wards were to fall
and leave our life
rebuilt on his.
The hospital
had nought to show
but scaffolding,
nothing beyond
the empty branch.
Winter zigzags
brought him outdoors,
no cold, no warmth,
from end to end.

In The Blizzard

I mind about
a tongue, made up
to be soundless,
it's imprinted
weeks from safety
like a memory.
What reminds us
how to speak it
is the brother
not receiving.
Without language,
he found sleeping,
spoke the silent
undertone. Here
another sleeps
but sideways, lost
to brotherhood
and early words,
too quiet yet
for sounding out.

***